Out from the Shadows, They Come

Four Stories

Kathleen Galvin Grimaldi

authorHOUSE®

AuthorHouse™
1663 Liberty Drive
Bloomington, IN 47403
www.authorhouse.com
Phone: 1 (800) 839-8640

Published by AuthorHouse   06/29/2017

ISBN: 978-1-5246-9194-3 (sc)
ISBN: 978-1-5246-9193-6 (e)

Print information available on the last page.

Any people depicted in stock imagery provided by Thinkstock are models, and such images are being used for illustrative purposes only. Certain stock imagery © Thinkstock.

This book is printed on acid-free paper.

Because of the dynamic nature of the Internet, any web addresses or links contained in this book may have changed since publication and may no longer be valid. The views expressed in this work are solely those of the author and do not necessarily reflect the views of the publisher, and the publisher hereby disclaims any responsibility for them.

Marianna Knowles
Kathleen Murnion
Joseph Grimaldi

I am grateful beyond words. Without the three of you, no book.

And a special *Thank You*

the Brett clan
on both sides of the Atlantic
for keeping the story
of John's tree alive

Harold Wilshinsky
who shared so much
of his mother Sadie's spirit
with me,
time and time again

Pete and Georgianna
for your time, suggestions,
laughter, dinners,
and endless patience

Ida Rabinowitz
for telling me a story
all those years ago
that I could never forget...

Poetry Collections by Author:
like smoke rising, like wind, Author House, 2011
Life's Glorious Song, Author House, 2015

Contents

Dedication

Out
from the shadows,
they come...

All shapes and sizes,
men women children
walk run stumble
their way to the deck,
catapulting forward
toward gang planks
extending like arms
over water
to welcome them
to the safety of land.

They made it.
Some with nothing more
than what they wore,
others -
a tattered valise
at their sides,
all with spirits weary and bruised
from the leave-taking:
family, friends, home, country.

Tired,
they have emerged
along with their dreams,
utterly surprised by survival.

Introduction

You and I were born here. But somewhere behind us, there was someone who made a choice to come to America. And coming, paid for our ticket ahead of time. What follows are four of those stories. Like many of you, I was raised on accounts of how my family had left the world of their birth and emigrated here. As an adult, I heard similar excerpts from friends about their families of origin. Facts always told me about what they did and when they did it. For me, there always seemed to be something else to look at, that if examined, would make that history come alive.

Take, for example, the account of the Pilgrims. All of us were told of their journey and the first Thanksgiving. But if I had been living back then in a cramped dwelling, not free to do much about my life, not even worship the way I chose to like so many others in my village, would I have been one who said - *Enough. I'm going to set out to sea with these brave souls, hope for the best, and find a place to start over*; or would I have been the neighbor next door, just as fed up, but not even considering that there might be an alternative, not being able, for quite a variety of justifiable reasons, to reach up and grab onto a choice that could carry quite serious consequences if things didn't work out? The facts that make up accounts, whether from history or our own family's history, don't always provide enough for us to imagine how we would respond in such a situation. And that's the one question that has always interested me.

A story, on the other hand, can have a different aim: to present to readers' imaginations real people trying to survive through the circumstances of their lives. Just the way we do with ours.

The following stories are based on people stepping out from my family's history and the histories of people I know. They show choices made by young people, maybe even your age. Their backgrounds are the late nineteenth century (1800's) and early twentieth century (1900's) with ages ranging from teen-age years (although that term wasn't used yet) to mid-twenties. This is the time period when we are told by those who know such things that the all - important question rises for the first time to the surface for most of us: *What do I want to do with my life?*

As I began reading background histories for each of these young people, I learned to admire the quiet courage that each one showed in making the choices they did. I started to wonder about how these choices found them. How did they find a way to step off the path they were walking on, starting all over again in a brand new world?

They lived in times quite different from our own: no cell phones or computers or television or widespread use of automobiles. But if we take a closer look, we can see that some problems in today's world were clearly present in theirs as well.

War has always been a shaper of so many lives. It certainly was then and continues to be today. A second problem was the lack of employment opportunities. Sound familiar? There were many more farms than exist today, and large families were the norm. Often these farms went to the eldest son. High school education constituted higher education, and this applied only for the select few who had the money available. It was the rare daughter who dreamed of a life back then, other than as someone's wife, but they could be found. America and what it promised held a history of appeal for dreamers of a different life. It always had. Finally, wherever one chooses to look in history, there have always been those whose personalities set them apart from the other lives around them. Those who were born with a vague discontent coursing through their veins like blood, always wondering about the adventure of Life along with just the living of it.

I have written these stories for readers like you, with family histories of your own, perhaps with faded photographs to go along with them. I hope that after meeting John, the serious thinker; Eric, so focused and determined; the irrepressible Sadie; and the tenacious young woman, Genia - you will be inspired to take a second look at the stories that have gone into shaping your own lives. Who knows what you will find there!

Oh Ireland, dear old Ireland
Will I ever see you more?
My very heart is aching to revisit
Thy green shores.
My very heart both night and day
Will ever long to see
The dear home in Kiltullagh,
The dearest place to me.

For thirty years an exile
In a foreign land I roam.
My memory oft reminds me of
My childhood's happy home.
And of those days I once enjoyed
When I was young and free
In the old home in Kiltullagh,
The dearest place to me.

I left that home when I was young
And always did maintain
A hope that in some future time
I would return again.
If fortune ere did favor me
I would go back to see
The old home in Kiltullagh,

The dearest place to me.

O where are all my comrades
Oh where are they today?
The comrades that I dearly loved
With whom I oft did play.
It's many a good old time we had
A rambling gay and free
Through the green fields of Kiltullagh,
The dearest place to me.

Now may God be with old Ireland that's many an exile's prayer and God be with Kiltullagh, my happiest days were there.

John J. Brett, 1912

John Brett
age 23
1881
Galway, Ireland

My mother, Margaret Brett Galvin,
was John's youngest daughter and
a natural story teller, one of which
was how her father came to America.

John's Tree

Michael Brett's whole body heaved as he sobbed into the tall green grasses alongside his wife Anna's grave in the small family cemetery. Lying face down, resting his head on his arms outstretched along the damp ground, he couldn't quite breathe in what had just happened to his life. Barely three years had passed since he had first laid eyes on her at the ceili held at his uncle's house. It was her laugh that he had heard first, and turned to see her with those deep golden curls dancing in the set of eight dancers closest to the door. Their eyes met, and he spent the next few sets finding his way to that side of the room. Shy, but personable by disposition, this lanky, dark-haired man was taken by surprise. *This is a first, for sure*, he half-muttered to himself.

Well, it took you long enough to find your way to the better half of the room, she teased him as he approached. *I'm Anna.*

They stepped outside into the crisp autumn air and never did make it back inside...

In the year 1860 in Cahernalea, Galway, along the western coast of Ireland, his wife, dear Anna, and two still-born sons had just been laid to rest, not even twenty-four hours ago. He could still hear the heavy clink of metal against stone as the grave site had been hastily dug in readiness for the burial, followed by the soft thump of the freshly dug earth being thrown back over the casket by those gathered around. As the shadows of the day lengthened and the winds coming in along the coast-line picked up their speed, the last of the visitors were leaving the cemetery. All except Michael.

How had his life come to this? How? Why, God, why? were words that had become a mantra for him now.

⸺ ⸺ ◉ ⸺ ⸺

Michael and most of his family had emerged unscathed by the diseases brought about following the terrible years of the blight begun in 1845 and continuing until 1850. Michael knew even then that he would never forget the stench-filled fog that settled in preceding the fungus-like attack on the potatoes. That same weather affected the livestock as well, causing the number of sheep and pigs to fall dramatically. The impact had been wide, disastrous.

But in time the good Lord had sent him Anna, and, like their parents before them, they worked hard to start a life for themselves. Little John, born in 1858, had already brought laughter into their days. *So much like his mother with that honey-colored hair and those blue, blue eyes,* Michael would think to himself. In typical Irish fashion, his good fortune scared him at times. Then catastrophe struck.

One minute he and Anna were laughing at the table over something John was attempting to say, and the next minute she had collapsed and bade him ride to the nearest farm for help. He returned to find young John asleep on the floor, and Anna, close by, near death.

Promise me to leave here, Michael. Start over again with John. Find a way to be happy.

And just like that, his Anna was gone.

In 1863, Mary Fahey, whose parents had known Michael and his family, agreed to marry him and move to a farm in Kiltullagh, still in Galway, but far enough away for new memories to take hold. So soon after the birth of Ellen, all four set off for the farm where the rest of John's half-siblings (fourteen in all) would be born over the next twenty years.

But it was John who would remain closest to his father's heart. In many ways through the intervening years John would seem an enigma to him, this only surviving son of Anna Scully, his first love. Her eyes, so blue, always were shining back to him from this man-child's face, and her love of words was taking shape in the teacher he was now becoming. Michael watched distance settle into young John's personality as he grew older. *His mind always seems so far away,* Michael would catch himself thinking. *Ah that's the poet in him for sure,* Michael half-laughed to himself on more than one occasion when he would observe young John gazing out over the farm lands, his lanky long arms resting on the top of a shovel or hoe.

John always could sense when his father was worried about him. *Maybe I remind him of my mother. He's always telling me how she felt about things, this country that she loved so much - a rebel was how he jokingly referred to her on more than one occasion.*

If you only knew, Da, if you only knew...

In 1880 farm lands were once again in distress, particularly in the west of the country. The Great Famine still loomed as a giant specter in the imaginations of the generations living now. Families had been torn apart, and the ever-present fear was that it could so easily happen again. This was the year that the names Charles Parnell and Michael Davitt became strongly associated with the Land League. Both were dedicated to bettering the position of tenant farmers, hoping to eventually redistribute the land among them.

In a flash, John's imagination took him back to the first time he had laid eyes on Parnell. By chance, he had accompanied a neighbor, Terence McCarthy, into town to help him out with forms that needed filing.

These English, always wanting something else from us poor souls. Not bad enough that almost all our crops are set up for export, profit going to England - thank you very much!

John had watched as the elder McCarthy became more and more agitated, probably due to the difficulty this man had with any printed material. For so many of his generation, reading and writing were luxuries not easily afforded. That's why he and his wife insisted on *book learning* for their sons, at least.

Mr. McCarthy, I can go with you into town if you like. Two heads are better than one, my Da always says.

And so they had arrived just when Parnell was being escorted into the town hall to address those who had assembled there.

Do you mind, sir, if I listen in while you take care of your other business? We can do the necessary forms first if you like at the Post Office. Then give me a time to meet up with you at the pub later...

The elder McCarthy hesitated. He knew how concerned Michael Brett was about John.

We can keep this between you and me, can't we? John posited. *And the drinks at the pub, on me.*

That will stay between us, too - I give you my word.

John was old enough to know that most wives (Mrs. McCarthy, no exception) always warned their men against stopping off at the pub.

He remembered how he had stood in the back, trying to blend into the dark paneling that lined most county buildings. *No wonder Parnell is appealing to so many,* he had thought to himself at the time. *He knows how to stir the blood of Irishmen. Must be like the patriots of Young Irelandism that Da never tires telling me about in his father's day, most of whom were shipped off to Australia, never to be back in Ireland again. Cruelty to be sure,* John thought to himself. Yet somehow his grandfather and his Da, and so many others like them, found their survival by following what they were told to do.

*I don't know if I'm made that way...*was the uncomfortable thought weaving its way through John's mind as he quietly

11

exited before Parnell's speech was over to keep his appointment at the pub.

In the months that followed, John found himself increasingly pre-occupied with the words of Parnell, the blazing logic presented speech after speech about home rule. Here and there he would meet up with others of like mind, partly due to his part - time work as an itinerant teacher.

Pay attention, John, he would remind himself. *Stay in the shadows. Don't let anything get back to Da. I don't think he could bear it if I were to be taken away.*

Every once in a while, he found himself thinking of all his siblings. What was life going to be like in their futures? So many of them were almost a younger generation. What were their chances for an education? On some level, Da must be thinking along the same lines by seeing that money was always put aside for my schooling. He could see in his mind's eye that white enameled cup that sat on top of the cabinet in the kitchen. It was understood that every spare coin went into it for his schooling. No discussion.

No, he would do nothing to draw attention to himself.

1881

The lamplight burned steadily from the kitchen table where Michael and John often sat after dinner had been cleared away.

More than the others, he can feel the land the way I do - its rolling green fields and fertile farmlands. Maybe that's what leads him to pen and paper when chores are done. He gets a second wind somehow... Michael mused, *that and the reading of book after book.*

John, I understand the reading of books, but why a dictionary of all things? Who ever heard of that?

John stopped, looked up and smiled back at his Da, shrugged his shoulders, and went back to his reading. He was being molded not only by these books, but by the times in which he lived, and the hopes that were being raised in the hearts of tenant farmers everywhere.

Da, he had argued with his father more than once, *we have a right to at least some of what our labor produces and maintains. Why should it all go to England? Any farmer should see the absolute sense of that!*

Michael was an intelligent man, yet simple and focused as to where he would extend his energies. Providing food for his family and a safe roof over their heads, that was enough for him. Anything that extended beyond that frame of reference to include all of Ireland with a future different from its past was not part of who he was. He was beginning to realize, however, that it was becoming part of his son's identity, and so like dear Anna before him. The famine had seen so many flee and set out for places all over the globe. The times were growing differently now. Leaders were being shaped as surely as the crops that he worked so hard to grow. On some level, Michael knew that John would be one of them.

John withheld a lot from his father. He had secretly joined the Land League when it formed in 1879, going against what he knew to be his father's wishes. He bantered back and forth with him over what he saw in town, even getting him to laugh once in a while over a joke one of the McCarthy's had told him. He didn't want to worry this man who worked so hard. He was getting on in years now. But John couldn't help but be drawn into the dream of Home Rule that Charles Parnell, the current leader of the Land League, represented to him and other young idealistic men. Here was a man young like himself and so many others, but hardened and focused on an Irish government being led by Irish men on Irish soil. Although Parnell was a Protestant land owner, he was also the son of an American mother who carried a heritage of political freedom and equality coursing through the blood in her veins. No doubt her son Charles inherited his share of that same blood. John traveled along the hedge rows that dotted the countryside as an itinerant, or hedge teacher, as they were commonly called, and learned a great deal about what was happening throughout Ireland, helping circulate necessary information to others of like mind. He had to be careful. The League was being watched. He couldn't afford to be found out.

Da looks worried, John thought to himself as he lifted his head from his books. *Why don't you call it a day, Da, and turn in? The rooster will be crowin' before ya know it...*

The elder Brett pushed back his chair from the table, leaned over John's work, and patted his son's shoulder as he rose.

You're right, son. All my bones are agreein' with ya one by one. See ya in the mornin'...

John watched him fade into the shadows as he left the kitchen for the back of the house.

No man of his age should have to work the land as hard as he does for so little.

John didn't know it, but thoughts such as these were fanning the fire of a growing unrest within him. The elder Brett had a right to be worried.

—◁ ···· ▸◦◁ ···· ▷—

Time passed easily into weeks as the longer days grew warmer. Planting time always left John as tired as his Da because most days didn't end in the fields. The longer light at day's end found him taking his horse to one or two neighboring farms for lessons. Those further away like the O'Shaughnessy's and McCarthy's were best served on the weekends. The children at these farms were older, too. They were the ones wanting to know about Parnell and what was happening in Dublin.

Walk a fine line, John, he reminded himself as he tried to answer the questions being asked of him, especially what he knew about the Fenians. John never forgot that the Fenian movement was founded the same year he was born - 1858. *Surely that means something,* he often thought to himself. First Young Irelandism, then Fenianism: just different names for the same thing, home rule. Ireland making her own rules for her own people. A cry across generations now. It would be from this parent organization that the Irish Republican Brotherhood would eventually be spawned, and, in time, the IRA, which is still part of Ireland's current political landscape.

This group was too radical in its beliefs for most farmers. Their teen-age sons, though, another story...

One such boy was Terence McCarthy. John always looked forward to working with this inquisitive red-head. Like John, he worked hard alongside his father and brothers, but they all knew time had to be spared for Terence's lessons. Resentful or not, they knew how smart he was. University had to be etched into his future. He was their only hope for a better life.

John knew something was wrong when he arrived early that Saturday afternoon at the McCarthy farm. No Terence at the table, only the two younger boys.

Where's your brother? John queried as he set the boys up with their lessons.

He went with Da into town this morning. Usually they're back by the time you get here, though, responded Davy, the smaller of the two. Cieran, the quieter one, went to the window.

*Here he comes now, but Da's not with him. He's riding one of the horses back. Something must have happened to Da...*With that, he bounded out the door and down the long path to meet his brother as he came over the ridge into view again.

Get John for me, Terence yelled to Cieran as he galloped up to the porch.

By now, John and the younger boy stood in the doorway.

Cieran, take your brother inside while I talk to John.

Neither one of the younger boys even considered offering a reply. Off they went.

John, Da told me to get back to you as fast as I could manage. When he went into the Post Office, he overheard the Guarda talking among themselves about Parnell. He's been arrested and taken to Kilmainhaim Jail in Dublin. But what really upset him was he thought he heard your name mentioned as one of Parnell's workers in the field. Someone argued against it, but Da couldn't tell who was saying what. He thinks they'll probably send someone after ya...if Parnell was thrown into prison and threatened with execution, what about others? Da slowly unhitched one of the horses and told me to get to you...

You don't have much time, John. Here's the boat schedule from Queenstown to America. Da said to tell you 'Don't think. Say good-bye and go.' They're ready to lynch just about anybody.

By now, Mrs. McCarthy came out to the porch, burying John in one of her huge embraces. Forcing a bag with two apples and some bread and cheese into his hands, she gave him the reins to his horse. *Get yourself back to your Ma and Da, make your good-byes, leave the horse with them, and set out by foot for Queenstown. It might take you close to a week to get there, but you can take cover more easily if you have to, if you're on foot rather than horseback. Besides, your folks can come up with some excuse for your whereabouts if your horse is still here.*

John concentrated on the steady clop - clop of his mare's hoofs along the dirt road back to Kiltullagh. How could he leave here? His mind drew pictures of the hearthside in early evening when all his younger siblings would scramble for their tablets and pencils and a seat close to him. Little Thomas, only two, would crawl under the table to sit on his foot. John could almost hear the impish laughter now. *They're probably why I have always seen myself as a teacher. Who else has thirteen siblings and still counting? After all, little Bernard Joseph has only just been born!* To many of the brood, he was a grown-up, and knew just about all there was to know. How could he ever leave these siblings that seemed more like his own children? He was an old twenty-three for sure, an *old soul* his step-mother teasingly called him. How dear she was, the only mother he had ever known. He loved the farm; he had never thought of life being lived anywhere else. *Just until things settle a bit*, he told himself. *Then I can come back...*

Nothing seemed real. He finished off one apple, stuffing the core and seeds into his pants pocket. Not even aware of what he was doing, he began chomping down the second.

It must have been the pallor of his complexion or maybe it was the drone-like quality to his voice as he spoke. No one questioned him as he told them what he had to do. All eyes were on him, just staring. Never had they been this quiet or this still. He couldn't bring himself to look directly at his father. No one moved when he grabbed his worn pouch to fling over his shoulder. It was clear to him that his father had hastily stuffed bills under its flap.

It was then that little Mary, only five, ran to stand in the doorway, her arms folded in front of her like her mother's when she was about to be scolded: *You can't leave us, John - you can't.*

When he picked her up and tried to hand her over to his father, her little fists kept trying to pummel him. Giving up, she half - sobbed:

Come back, John - come back, PROMISE!

How he made it out the door without looking back, he never could quite remember. He was almost to the gate when he stopped and turned.

He scanned the landscape in front of him. Impulsively, he reached into his pants pocket and retrieved the apple seeds he had placed there less than an hour ago.

Walking back to the side yard near the stone house, he hastily grabbed the shovel that was always leaning against the shed. He began digging a hole as if his life depended on it. In a way, it did.

I'm planting these seeds, he said to no one in particular. *And when a tree grows, let it be, so I can see it when I return.*

With that, he waved once more, and set out for Queenstown.

John made it to America, and in time, bought a farm in New England. He never made it back to Kiltullagh. Two generations later, another John Brett (Galvin), his grandson, did make it back to see the tree grown from those seeds, standing behind a simple sign saying, *John's Tree.*

---

for my brother Brett
who shares the legacy...

Family/Historical Facts

- Young Irelandism, Fenianism, Land League - Irish social movements of the 19th century springing from the desire for home rule, rather than being subjects of the English government
- Charles Parnell, Michael Davitt - leaders
- John Brett - a hedgerow teacher before emigration
- He left Ireland the same year Parnell was imprisoned - 1881*
- He left quickly after being told that his name had been given to British authorities by an informer
- He planted apple seeds before he left with the instruction to let a tree grow - John's Tree
- He continued to support the Land League from America
- Even into advancing age, he could be found reading pages from the dictionary - and telling the story of Charles Parnell
- At the time of Queen Victoria's visit in 1849, the ancient city of Cobh was renamed Queenstown in her honor. In 1950, it reverted back to its former name.

* Charles Parnell was released from prison in 1882 (the year following John's emigration) His great achievement was to place Home Rule firmly on the agenda of English politics.

Author's Note:

Facts are the building blocks for any history to reveal itself to future generations. Often, however, the links connecting them one to the next are lost over time.

The author has taken the liberty of presenting one possible way these facts could have unfolded, one after another...

Sadie Redish
age 15
1917
Chodorov, Austria

I first heard of Sadie through
her grand-daughter,
Karen Wilshinsky Griffiths. When I
heard her words - "I'm not such a good
girl, I'll travel alone to America" -
I knew I wanted to tell her story!

"I'm not such a good girl. I'll travel alone to America."

The year was 1914 and change swirled through the air surrounding events in the tiny village of Chodorov on the outskirts of Lemberg, Austria where Benjamin Redisch lived with his wife Rose and their six children. The history of this place had always been one of tolerance; but recent events, at least to the Jewish population, were slowly calling this tradition into question. Benjamin's family had lived here for generations, and he loved being a part of that history.

Why he could remember as a child walking to his grandfather's, stopping by the cemetery to spot the tall stone with Redisch carved so deliberately in stately Hebrew script standing apart from the smaller stones to either side. He could remember how the sun's rays would cast beams from the indentations in the stone; he was a part of that line stretching back into a larger history.

Then there was the memory of market days. How he had loved traveling with his grandfather into town where each wagon carried different goods, mostly crops from nearby farms, and wheat everywhere! The commercial streets were a bonus on days when they had sold all their wares. He and his grandfather would travel from one shop to another along the tree-lined streets. So many people with the sounds of animals and laughter and bargaining all wrapped into one glorious welcome rising to meet a young child's ears. The sameness of those days wrapped around him even now like a warm blanket designed to keep out the encroaching cold.

Memories such as these committed him to the traditions of his family. He would live and die here like all the Redisches before him. But as events were beginning to unfold, he no longer felt as certain that this would be the destiny for his children.

All Benjamin's neighbors would readily agree that he was a hard-working man and had always been one. His hands betrayed him - a nick here, a cut there from harnessing the often reluctant horses before setting off for town gave the appearance of a man much older than he was. He worked as a courier for the various banks which brought him into contact with the nearby villages and the larger city of Lemberg. He also managed a dairy route, so he often was the first to hear of what was happening in the larger world.

His face carried the well-worn lines of worry that were not just unique to him, but to heads of Jewish households throughout the area. Slowly but surely, anti-Semitic rumors were surfacing even as far north as Chodorov. Trusted friends coming back from cities further west or south would tell of a curfew here or damage to property there.

No one could forget the stories that had circulated throughout the nearby villages back in 1905 when it was rumored that over 400 Jews had been killed with over 1600 homes damaged almost beyond repair in Odessa. Some rumors put the numbers as high as 2500! He had almost succeeded over the years in dismissing such a thought, though - how could that possibly be true? Benjamin followed the politics of the day. There was unrest in Germany to the west and in Russia to the east. He knew, deep down, that something was astir.

He had also begun to feel change closer to him in small ways: the sudden loss of a customer, a sharp word from another. People he had known all his life seemed to be changing right in front of him. His cousin Aaron had pointed this out years before when he set out for America soon after he had saved enough money to book passage.

This second-class citizenship is not for me, he had uttered.

And he had been right. Countless were the times that Benjamin found himself ruminating over his cousin's words as he traveled back and forth into Lemberg. *Jobs are like diamonds in the streets,* Aaron had said more than once in his letters back to Austria. Aaron's recent letters were growing more urgent. It almost seemed as though Aaron knew more about what was going on in Europe than Benjamin knew, living there. Maybe all of them should emigrate to America? Aaron had suggested this more than once. Out of the question, as far as he was concerned, but he found himself telling Rose about Aaron's comments.

When Benjamin had brought up the idea to Rose, she had posed the hard questions: *How can I leave my parents behind just when they are about to need me? They could never make such a trip and survive, even if they wanted to. And our oldest about to marry? All he is thinking about is settling down and beginning his own family here in Chodorov like all the Redisches before him. How can we deny him that? isn't that how we raised him? I know there's unrest, but there has always been that. We'll just deal with it the best we can like we've always done...*

And the issue would be dropped for the time being. Once in a while, when work was slow, Benjamin would catch himself thinking: *What if armies ever were to march through here? What would happen to my beautiful daughters?* Sarah came first to mind being the older - the dream-like quality to her blue eyes, her shining hair, her almost regal posture, her quiet ways. Then Sadie - that irrepressible spirit always hiding right behind her eyes, laughing its way through just in the way she would look at you, the incessant chatter...he shuddered these worries away like someone shooing away a bothersome fly.

Oh Benjamin, Rose would say to him when she would catch him lost in thought. *It's not all that bad, you'll see...*

And he would rest easy for a time. He longed for her to be the one with her pulse on the reality of things here, not his cousin so far away from them both in distance and in circumstance.

The day the letter arrived containing the ticket to America was like any other day in my life. I remember that I had awakened early, as soon as sunlight flooded into the small attic room I shared with my sister Sarah. The sunlight always lit her half of the room first, but with her back to the window and the pillow pulled over her head, most mornings she was still asleep after the sun rose.

Not me. Most days I couldn't wait to get going. Especially that day. Papa was taking an extra trip into Lemberg. How I so wanted to go along! Something was always happening there. The smells alone while traveling along Market Street with all its vendors hawking their wares, especially the ones you could pick up with your hands and just gobble in one gulp. Depending upon his mood, Papa sometimes gave me a few coins for a special treat, but always with the warning given with a twinkle in his eyes: *Don't you dare tell your mother now!*

Sometimes if he had business to conduct with another merchant he would let me go off on my own. Those were the best of times. I could worm my way in and out among the various stalls, fingering some fabric in one place or tasting a sample of something scrumptious in another. It's always like tasting freedom! Surely this must be what America is like...

Cutting into my own thoughts, I bounced out of bed and grabbed my robe. Today I needed to be fast. Everything would depend upon Mama. I could hear her inside my head: *Now Sadie, slow down. What's your hurry? The windows would have far fewer streaks after you've washed them if you just would take more time...*

My response would always go something like this: *Oh. Mama - what's a streak or two? I so want to go with Papa into Lemberg.*

And it would start between the two of us. Sarah hated the city, so I would suggest letting her fix the one or two streaks left behind. Then Sarah would chime in and Mama would throw up her hands and say, *Handle it yourselves.* If there was one thing I was good at, it was handling Sarah. Only one and a half years apart in age, we couldn't have been more different.

Sarah was beautiful; everybody said so. At seventeen, boys would trip over each other to get to carry her packages or walk her to services. And she always smiled so sweetly at them all. Me? I could care less about boys. I was always interested in helping Papa; he was the one who went to the city. Ever since I could remember when he made it home at dinnertime he would talk to us about what was happening in Lemberg. *Rose, you should see the new style hats women are wearing. And their hair styles are changing too. Little circles on either side above their ears...*

And I would imagine what it would be like to live in a city and change styles every season or two. Maybe that's why talk of America always filled my imagination so with what it would be like to go there. And I would imagine that no one was poor like here. Don't get me wrong; we were poor, but elegant - as Mama would often say. We always had music to sing and dance to, which we did every chance we got.

I'm sorry for digressing - back to that day. I remember thinking as I picked up the brush on my dresser and smiled into my reflection in the mirror: *How best to approach you today, Mama?* The face that looked back at me was nothing like my mother's. I remember thinking that at least I got the hair color right. I really couldn't blame my mother for getting so exasperated with me...

I closed the door quietly behind me. I knew it would be a window day and that I would bribe Sarah with promises to do her share of the dishes for the rest of the week. But I would still need to convince Mama.

With that, I remember forcing myself to come down the stairs one at a time, just like a lady should, just what would put me on Mama's good side for the morning.

I loved the way you could always smell the city before the first buildings came into view in the distance, especially in the warmer months. Animal smells were the first, a mixture of horse manure and chickens. As we passed the farms the smell of cows certainly got our noses ready for what was to come. The countryside here in Austria was truly beautiful - rolling fields that seemed to stretch on forever dotted with fruit trees here and there especially further away from the well-traveled roads. But those smells reminded you that a different world was approaching, a busier one filled with so much more than the quiet roads we were now on. I think it was probably the anticipation that I always felt that began my dreaming of the streets of America. Another world was beginning to take shape within me, like these different smells signaled the approach to a larger world, while I sat here alongside Papa.

We always stopped at the Post Office as soon as we came into the city's center. *You stay here, Sadie, and mind the store,* he would always say to me as he handed over the reins and bounded off the wagon. As soon as he went through the doors, I would hitch the horse to the small railing along the street's edge and walk across the street and halfway up the same stairs that he had climbed just moments before. I loved being able to look out in all directions. No matter where I looked, there was something to feast my eyes on: people in all shapes and sizes, colors like a vast rainbow stretching from one end of the center to the other, clothing so different from what was seen in the countryside. And hats! Everyone wore hats, it seemed - women and men alike. Not everyone was Jewish here, and you noticed it first through the clothing and the way both women and men wore their hair. How I loved seeing all the differences! *Back to the wagon, Sadie,* I reminded myself. It would never do for Papa to come out and find me on the steps. I had just about returned to my spot when he came out holding only one letter.

This is odd, he half-muttered to himself. *It's a letter from my cousin Aaron, but it's addressed to Sarah.*

With that, he placed it in his vest pocket and we continued on our way.

That night at dinner, I couldn't wait for Papa to give Sarah the letter. I knew better than to keep asking about it. As soon as I cleared away the dishes, I hurried back from the kitchen when I saw him place the letter on the table.

Sarah, this letter arrived for you from my cousin Aaron.

How different we were. Me? I would have snatched the letter before it was placed down in front of me, ripping it open all in one movement. Not Sarah. She carefully unsealed the envelope, read silently the short note inside, and placed a ticket to America on the table.

Cousin Aaron says that his family is in need of a housekeeper since the girl that they had employed is leaving the city. Because I am the oldest daughter, he thought he would offer the position to me. He understands, Papa, that you don't feel you can take the whole family and leave here as he has suggested. He respects your decision, even though he thinks it is the wrong one, and hopes you don't mind his offering this opportunity to me, just the same...

No one said anything. I remember so well how loud the silence sounded to my ears. Sarah fingered the corner of the ticket for what seemed a very long time. Then she stood up, bringing the ticket with her over to Papa and placed it down in front of him, saying:

Good girls don't travel alone to America. I don't want to go.

Without thinking, I jumped up from my place and snatched the ticket as soon as she placed it down.

Good. I'll go. I'm not such a good girl. I'll travel alone to America.

Benjamin knew enough not to challenge her, this lively one so dear to his heart. Always restless, she seemed to have her sights set on bigger things. So when Sadie grabbed the ticket from the table, daring him with her eyes to stop her, he knew he couldn't.

Papa, I'm a hard worker and can think on my feet and learn quickly, you've said so yourself, Papa. Cousin Aaron will let me stay with him and his family just the way Sarah was going to. I can't wait, Papa. America is just so special. I can't wait until I'm older.

31

He couldn't take his eyes off her, this one so sure of her life going forward, so confident that she could handle whatever would find itself on her path. And somewhere deep inside him, he knew that most likely she would. But let her go? Almost certain never to see her again? How does a parent find the strength to consent to that? But like Aaron's father before him when Aaron left, and those fathers yet to come, all of them just want their children to be happy.... so Sadie was going to America.

The next few weeks were a whirlwind. There was no time to think, and perhaps that was a good thing as far as Sadie was concerned. All she focused on was this dream of hers that had, like a miracle, appeared on her doorstep. She was oblivious to her mother's watery eyes every time they rested on her younger daughter and the times that Sarah took up her chores without being asked or her father brought home a little something to pack away for the trip. The biggest surprise of all was her brothers - Benjamin, Morris, and David, the youngest, who kept following her around and asking her when she would be coming home from her big trip. They actually were nice to her, offering to take her to town on an off day in case she had something to purchase. Suddenly everyone seemed to be a stranger. That's when it began to take shape in her heart, the finality of this decision she had snatched from the dining room table just a few weeks before. Maybe one of life's dearest blessings to the young is their keen sense of immortality sweeping them forward with their dreams. In any case, even though Sadie could feel on some level the sadness in everyone else's heart, it didn't come close to placing a shadow on her own. The sheer excitement of it all was carrying her through.

When the day of departure finally arrived, everything seemed unreal, playing itself out in slow motion. Of course, her father was the one to take her to the train in Lemberg. To date, that city had been the boundary of her world. Now a train would take her to a ship departing from Hamburg, Germany for America's shores. As she watched her father take down her valises to place them on the cart for the train, Sadie noticed for the first time how stooped his shoulders were becoming. *My father is getting old,* she surprised herself in thinking. *Somehow I never thought of him or Mama as ever getting old.* As he came back to her side, Sadie readied herself for the good-bye that would have to last her the rest of her life.

As for Benjamin, he put out his arms and she found her way in, just the way she had ever since she was a child. Where had all that time gone? Soon she would be gone, too.

Remember, my dear Sadie, as wonderful as this dream of America is for you, remember the stones on the ground there are not kosher. Do not forget you are Jewish. He had kept from all of them what Aaron had confided to him in his letters. Anti-Semitism didn't stop at the water's edge, but its consequences weren't as severe on the other side. One could still build a life if one worked hard and made use of opportunities that were all around. Benjamin was counting on this. Of all his children, she was the one he could most easily see finding her way forward with both feet planted firmly on the ground ahead of her, even though she was young. Hard as this was, he wouldn't stand in her way.

Sadie half-sobbed her words into the thickness of his coat that always felt to her like a warm blanket of safety. *I won't forget what you've taught me, Papa. I will remember to fast the Monday after I arrive in thanksgiving. I promise, Papa.*

Benjamin stood there after she boarded. He stood there until he could no longer see her hand waving good-bye from the small window, until the train itself disappeared from view, taking his Sadie into a much larger world than his beloved Chodorov. Only then did he turn around to find his way back to a life that would no longer have Sadie sitting to his right at the dining room table.

As soon as I saw the ship, I swear my heart skipped a beat or maybe it just started beating faster in my chest. As I started up the plank that would place me on board, I felt like I was climbing to the top of a mountain peak. People were pushing me along and up. Everyone was taller than I, or so it seemed. I found myself watching an older man and woman who had found themselves a space along the deck so they could watch as the ship left the port. I followed suit and squeezed into a space along the railing. There was something about the way the breezes blew across my face that calmed me, that enabled me to take a hard look at the city resting before me, knowing that most probably, I would never be back here. I kept looking until it was more and more of the grey sea that I was taking in, along with the matching clouds filling the skies above. Suddenly I was famished. I found a place against the inside wall and unpacked the crackers that were somewhat crumbled in my coat pocket. No matter. For now these would do just fine! For now, I just wanted to chew my crackers, lean my head back, and close my eyes. *You're doing it, Sadie. America is just out there...*

Voyagers traveled in three classes, I soon found out. I was third class or steerage, which was the roughest way to go. People were treated a lot like the cargo carried in windowless compartments deep in the lower spaces of these giant ships. I heard other passengers refer to it as being *down in the hole*. It was the lowest-priced way to travel to America, so there were many, many of us!

As soon as the ship was out on the open sea with no land anywhere in sight, the waters became very rough. I don't think my nostrils will ever forget the acrid smells of seasickness that filled the airless quarters where we slept. There was no way to escape the smells of vomit, spilled food, and diarrhea. To try and make it to the deck was nearly impossible. I heard the deckhands mention that some waves were as high as thirty feet! It was that constant rocking that made everyone so sick. The stormy North Atlantic took a heavy toll on all of us. Many memories from that time aren't clear in my mind, only flashes of fear (especially when the fog was very thick) and constant illness. I remember just lying on what served as a mattress. To get up meant to get so dizzy that you'd be sick to your stomach again because the waters were so rough. So many times I remember thinking to myself, *Surely the ship will turn over and spill us all out into the freezing water. I don't even know how to swim!* I had never tasted such raw fear. Over time, my mind is letting go of these nightmarish memories. I'm really grateful for that.

It was a cold day in January when the ship started into New York harbor. When I saw Manhattan appear with all those tall buildings, it looked like they were swimming on top of the water! I don't think I will ever forget seeing Lady Liberty as she came into view, standing on Bedloe's Island, holding up her right arm as a beacon for all entering New York from the sea. Papa had told me she was a gift from France to America, but the size of her - so tall- almost took my breath away. She was right here, almost standing in front of me! Sharp peaks dotted the landscape as we came through these blue waters to rest at a pier at the southern-most tip of the island. I felt so new, so strange, and so young, and I had never been away from home.

Here I was now, a farm girl who often tended cows for my father and had once in a while made a trip into what stood for city life in my part of the world. Most of the people walking the streets of New York would never have heard of Chodorov or Lemberg.

Suddenly the boat slowed measurably, and I was jolted back into the very real present. As soon as we docked at the pier, we had to get on a rather flat, large boat called a ferry and were taken to another island close- by, called Ellis Island.

My first step onto dry land was there. Everybody seemed anxious, worried, and looking like they didn't know what would happen next. I moved with the crowd, glancing up at this huge building with its arched windows and a canopy extending out from the center, which housed the Great Hall where I knew we were headed from all the talk around me.

Eventually we were led up to the main stairwell. I'll never forget that first impression - this huge, high room that seemed like a gigantic synagogue, and the sounds amplified from this gathering of people in all sorts of strange clothes, speaking all different languages, and all at the same time! For one quick moment, I felt like putting my hands over my ears and squeezing my eyes shut so I could think. But our guide ushered us along toward some benches and we got our first meal - fish and big pitchers of milk, and bread.

When we had finished, we were led to an area on the second floor. At the top of the stairs, the first of a two-step medical exam took place. The doctors watched us as we approached singly, checking for lameness or some other physical deformity. Two doctors spent no more than two minutes with each of us. I remember when they checked our eyes, they turned our eyelids inside out. They especially looked for conjunctivitis. The unlucky ones couldn't proceed any further. It was so sad for these people, to have come this far and now - no further. There was also a place for delousing, if that was found to be necessary. I was one of the lucky ones; I could proceed to the next check point. An immigration inspector had a ship's manifest with him and information about me had been filled out by the ship's officer when I had boarded in Germany.

At this point, having passed my way through, I was free to board the ferry barge back to the Battery. I had been told someone who knew cousin Aaron would be holding a sign with my name and bring me by carriage to cousin's Aaron's house.

I really started to panic as I was almost thrown ashore when the barge pulled into the pier. People started to push from behind; I was practically catapulted on to land. Names were being called all around me - so much laughter and sobbing and hugging. I felt like I was marooned on an island. *Get it together, Sadie,* I tried hard to reassure myself. And then I saw it - the sign with Sadie written in dark black printer's ink. It looked so confident, this name of mine staring back at me, so assured that no other Sadie could possibly lay claim to it but me. Without realizing what I was doing, I began jumping up and down, waving my arms as wildly as I could in the young man's direction. He had looked so serious before he saw me, but then, he, too, broke into a grin, while signaling for me to make my way towards him.

I remember thinking to myself at that point, *O.K. Sadie, O.K. You finally made it to the streets of America...*

She held her head high, put one foot in front of the other, and marched over to the sign with her name. She was excited, but absolutely exhausted. As soon as the driver had strapped the luggage into place they were off. Her cousin lived in Brooklyn, but their ride started in Manhattan. Sadie didn't know where to look first. Suddenly she was wide awake again. The streetscape from the Battery across town was so vastly different from Lemberg. The first thing she noticed was the street itself, neatly quilted in brick and cobble. They went past elegant brownstones, some with arched windows, some with mansard roofs. She was absolutely astonished at the five-story brick and marble - faced Fifth Avenue Hotel.

This is a bit out of the way from where we are going, but I try to bring everyone here. No one has seen anything like it before. It makes up for what you've been through, don't you think? The driver half-turned to catch her eye as he narrated the story of the hotel.

She warmed to him immediately and the way he spoke. Somehow Sadie could get the gist of what he was saying as he spoke with his hands as well as his voice. Sadie was a quick learner and she vowed then and there to learn English as soon as possible. Smaller buildings and storefronts wainscoted in striped awnings were something to see. All the color! It wasn't long before Sadie was gaping at the ladies of fashion walking along the streets. Some skirts seemed supported by hoops that made them stand out from the shape of their bodies. Ribbon- trimmed hats made Sadie painfully aware of her own skirt now so tattered after the voyage. But she was too tired to be embarrassed and much too excited. Horse drawn trolleys passed them on both sides. By now they had crossed the recently opened Brooklyn Bridge and were headed down the street in Bedford-Stuyvesant where cousin Aaron lived. As she alighted from the carriage, she extended her gloved hand, ripped though it was, to this kindly man who had gone so much out of his way to show her a bit of what would now be her home. As he picked up the reins he tipped his hat, smiled, and was on his way.

I think New York is going to be just fine, just fine, Sadie sang to herself as she climbed the steps to her cousin's home.

The first thing that came to her mind was how huge everything was starting with the steps she had just climbed to reach the front door. As she waited for someone to come, she noticed the windows on both sides from the door. She counted eleven in all as her eyes swept each level. And plants to either side of the entrance made her think of the elegant homes she would see in the city with Papa, the ones he would drive her around to see when they had the extra time.

As soon as the door swung open, she knew that the tall robust man standing on the other side had to be her cousin. He had the same twinkle in his eyes that Papa had.

And here is our world traveler arriving right on our doorstep! his booming voice announced to whoever might be listening. One of his arms wrapped around her shoulders while his other bent slightly to pick up one of her bags. *Come in, come in. Get yourself out of New York's cold.*

With that she found herself standing in a room that reminded her of the waiting room at the train station. So large and yet it seemed to be only a place where you would take off your coat and hang it in a closet.

Well, everyone is just dying to meet you, Sadie. They're waiting in the front parlor. Are you up to this? With that, he came over and took her hand into his larger one. *You know I don't remember your mother all that well, but I do remember the color of her hair. Yours is exactly like hers, am I right?*

At the mention of her mother's name, Sadie's eyes immediately filled with tears. She was now so far away. In another world, really. Cousin Aaron hugged her again, this time patting her on the back saying:

There, there - no tears now. It will take time. You know that, don't you? We'll try to keep you busy so that your thoughts won't be running back to what you've left behind, but will begin to fill with excitement for this new world that you've been brave enough to come to. Enough said?

She stood back from this large man who in some ways reminded her of home and knew on some level that she was safe.

Come with me now to meet everyone. Rachel, who is closest in age to you, can't wait to meet you and have someone to share her room with. Her brothers Adam and Warren have always shared a room and now she can, too. Bede, our youngest, is only 3 months old, so she's only interested in her next bottle and having a dry bottom!

And with that, Sadie was ushered into the front room to meet her new family.

It wasn't long before my life settled into its new routine. Cousin Rebecca, Aaron's wife, probably thought that keeping me busy was the best way to fight off homesickness. Besides, I was filling a position here. I soon learned how much was expected of me. After all, they had sponsored my passage and offered me a home. Sunday would be the day I washed clothes for the whole family. Monday I would see to the ironing. Even though I was fifteen, back home I helped Mama; here, I did it all. Cousin Rebecca belonged to different groups throughout the city, and most days she would be volunteering or working at the orphanage. Tuesdays she stayed home longer than usual with the baby so I could do the food shopping. In the beginning she took me around to where I would be expected to travel on my own. The day she took me to see the Pennsylvania Station I couldn't believe what I was seeing! So much like the old Roman temples from history, she explained to me. I was really touched by how much she wanted me to see and learn from. One day we spent on what was called the lower East Side where we went all along Orchard Street from one little striped awning shop to another. One held nothing but fruit; I had never seen so many different kinds of fruit, some known to me, others, not. Another store would be the butcher's with chickens in little cages in the front and the sounds of butchering going on in the back where patrons weren't allowed.

My favorite storefront was where she would buy cousin Aaron's favorite little pastries reserved for Sabbath and special occasions. At home so much time had been spent making these treats in our own kitchen; Sarah and I had learned how to roll out the dough as soon as we were tall enough to reach over the table. I remember Papa had found a little stool for me to stand on that made it easier for me to keep up with Sarah. Not in America though. To think there was a place so close to where I lived where I could spend a whole morning going from shop to shop.

Another day she took me to Broadway and Tribeca just to visit. Here we saw more automobiles, but there were still plenty of horses and carriages, too. She told me that she felt sure in time with the trains and subways and now automobiles, most horses and carriages would disappear. One train even went under the Hudson River! I respected her for all she seemed to know about where life was heading. Both she and her husband were involved in so many things.

Learn to do as much as you can, Sadie. That helps so much with fitting in here in the city. So many people here aren't Jewish, don't observe our customs, or eat the foods that we eat. It's important that we sample their way of doing things, taste their foods. You'll love many of them!

I loved cousin Rebecca's enthusiasm! They had been in America for quite a while now and yet they still could get excited over new things crossing their paths, like the new Grand Central

Station that we visited on one of our excursions. That's what she called our jaunts together - excursions. I guess she missed the children all of whom except the baby were in neighborhood school. She explained to me that here in America that's what children did. It was the way they planned for a successful future.

...so you see how much I will need to depend on you Sadie, especially with the baby. Then when you have learned the language better, you can enroll in schooling for yourself at night. That's what many immigrants do here.

Wednesdays weren't my favorite. I was expected to wash all the windows throughout the five rooms. When she showed me how to avoid streaking, I couldn't help but think of Mama and Sarah. They would have been so much better at this than I was. But here I tried harder than at home. After all, I owed them my passage here and my room and board. Thursdays were set aside for the floors - all of them! I tried to go to bed early on Thursday nights; I was so tired out from that. Rachel would still have the light on doing her homework, but it didn't stop me from falling into a deep sleep as soon as my head hit the pillow. Even though we were close in age, we lived totally different lives. I really worked hard here, and Rachel seemed to be caught up in a life that I knew nothing about. On, Fridays, when I finished polishing the furniture I was allowed time for myself so I really developed a second wind. I would pick a place to explore. Once I traveled all the way to Central Park and just walked my way through the paths and woodlands. In a way it reminded me of the slower pace of my life back in Chodorov. I guess that's why I was drawn there. Saturdays were family days and I saw everybody then. We went to synagogue and enjoyed a big dinner earlier than usual. I so loved this time with everyone around. It reminded me so much of the family

I left behind. Papa and Mama were so faithful in writing to me. On Tuesdays I usually managed to mail a letter back home when I was out and about.

Being able to take myself all over the city did a lot to make me feel more at home. It wasn't enough to learn the language though. Depending on what section I found myself in, the spoken language changed. So many immigrants from so many different places. All were trying to learn a new language; all sounded different from one another, even though they were trying to say the same thing. I noticed they seemed to learn words that had something to do with what they sold or how much something cost. That's what gave me the most trouble in the beginning - the money. One of my cousins began teaching me the coins, the money I would use the most. At first, I declined his offer. He had seen me struggle over paying a delivery man. He had just come into the kitchen on a day he had stayed home from school.

He ran to my side at the door, taking the money from my hand. *Here let me.* With that, he counted out the exact amount for the delivery man and added another coin as well. *Here we give extra money when goods are brought to us,* he said to me as he nodded to the amused driver waiting to be on his way. I, too, found his imitation of his father's business-like demeanor entertaining, but I knew he was trying to help. So we began setting aside times when he would show me what he knew and it certainly helped. I tried not to have the older children observe us; I made it our little secret, and little Aaron seemed to love that. Being one of the youngest, he often wasn't taken seriously by his siblings, but I never forgot his kindness to me and how generous he was with his time. It was to him that I owed dropping my fears of venturing out and making my way. Whenever he was around, he would ask to come along. At first his mother hesitated, fearing he would slow me down or worse, get lost with me. Perhaps it was knowing I was responsible for him or perhaps it was trying to show off a bit for this trusting youngster, but in any case I gradually dropped being fearful in favor of looking forward to his constant chatter and company.

Because of his companionship on these occasions, I picked up more and more vocabulary. The routine of my days made me more confident in my ability to manage on my own. When I turned seventeen, I approached cousin Aaron. I wanted to go to night school and get a job outside his home so I could save money and find a place of my own to live.

I went to work on Delancey Street, but before long I got a job in a new factory that opened on Broadway and Canal Streets. I wasn't afraid of hard work; no immigrant was, as far as I could see. Before long I changed jobs so that I could earn $10 a week. I had to move to Harlem way uptown at 112th Street where I paid $6 a week board. I even took a second job and attended school one night a week. I had become good with money, spending sparingly and sending money back home when I managed to save $25. I remember my lunch was often two bananas, which cost one penny. Sure, I felt hungry some times, but who didn't?

As soon as Papa started to receive the money I had saved, he started in on me. *So Sadie, when are you going to get married?* At first I laughed when I read his words. I could almost hear him saying them to me with that light twinkle in his eyes that I missed seeing so much. I really was quite content living on my own, finding myself all around the city that I was growing to love. But each of his letters now would hold the same question. As soon as I started the sentence that began, *Now Sadie...* I knew what was coming.

So I got hold of a good guy and a married lady I became. I had managed to save $140 by the time we got married. My first victory as one was to convince my new husband, Max Wilshinsky, to let me open a fruit store for us both rather than to go on a honeymoon.

The years flew by. Babies came. Businesses opened, closed, and new ones were tried whenever we failed. I learned from my life as I lived it. I always told my children: *You must take care of your education. That is the key to succeeding, and maybe you won't have as much failure as we did.*

Their father was different from me in many ways, but I always supported him when he would tell his children: *You can't live your life looking behind you. There is only baggage there. Your future is where your life is. Invest in it.*

Tears would always come to my eyes when I heard him speak those words. His whole family had been killed by the Cossack army back in Russia when he was away. He, too, learned from his life.

Looking back, I know that is one thing that I did well. I invested completely in my life. If I had ever decided to write its story, I could have had a best seller on my hands! And to think it started when I picked up that ticket to America that Sarah placed in front of Papa all those years ago...

All things considered, maybe I was a good girl after all!

Sadie never returned to Chodorov or Lemberg. As far as is known, her entire family there perished at Auschwitz/Birkenau. Sadie and her husband had four children. One son, Harold, was part of a business group that purchased the one synagogue left standing near to the Birkenau death camps. He was also instrumental in the establishment of the Jewish Museum of New York and currently serves on its Board of Trustees.

Family/Historical Facts

- Sadie's words

- Redish family history; Jewish history at time

- General description of life aboard ship

- Description of Ellis Island, New York City – 1917

- Responsibilities upon arrival (many immigrants from many countries sponsored by extended family were expected to work in similar fashion)

- Account of Sadie's life, marriage

Author's note:

I have used Sadie's story to explore what it might have been like for a teen-age girl in the year 1917 trying to find her way forward in New York, beginning with first seeing Lady Liberty in the harbor.

Eric Gustav Fuhrmann
age 25
1924
Germany

Eric's son and daughter-in-law, Peter and Georgiana, are dear friends of mine. What is unique to this story is that, if happening today, Eric would be considered an "illegal alien". When I first heard this term used for immigrants today, Eric's story, and the idea for this book, started to take shape in my mind.

...a decision born of circumstance

The history books tell us how World War I toppled the four great empires of the Old World. Many of these same books give numbers for lives lost and maimed, homes and businesses destroyed, economies obliterated. It was as a result of this war that the face of Europe as we see it today started to become visible. New lines were drawn showing where one country now ended and another began. Like the dark lines in coloring books. Some countries large. Others small. Countries with new names. Or same names but different borders. Everything changed. What the books don't talk about is how the above translated into the everyday life of a young German lad in his twenties who saw villages along the German border disappear due to the incessant fires igniting day after day in a war that as yet had no name.

Eric Gustav Fuhrmann became part of a vast movement that took him into Belgium, the first time ever leaving Germany, the country where he was born in 1899.

At first the excitement of travel acted as a powerful lure pulling him like a magnet towards the unknown. Like so many other youth being called into service, he failed to note the worried look creeping into the warm eyes of his mother Anna as she listened to him that day as he told her of his hasty induction into Germany's army, and announced almost as an afterthought that he would be leaving the following day.

Keep your hands busy, this slight but sturdy woman told herself as she moved about the kitchen, first checking the oven, then returning to the floured board ready for the quick cutting of biscuits to accompany her son's last dinner before this army that he kept talking about swept him away from her, perhaps forever.

As she kept pushing the strands of graying hair away from her flushed face, she managed to return his gaze - she owed him this much. All he could see, she knew, was the chance to step one foot into the larger world that had been part of his chatter from the time he was old enough to toddle about the beer garden restaurant that she and her late husband had lived their lives in.

How he had loved it there, she mused, remembering how this fair-haired, blue-eyed youngster would chase his sister Marta inside and out through the stoned terraces usually vacant during the day. How she would howl when he succeeded in grabbing one or both of her braids as he got close to her. That usually would be when Anna would call them into the kitchen where she could keep an eye on them as she baked strudel for the daily desserts. When she would put the leftover dough wrapped in jelly on a plate for the two of them you would think they had found gold.

They were satisfied with such simple things back then. Was it really such a long time ago? she found herself thinking.

Her older son Alfred had changed overnight that year her husband Gustav had died suddenly. She still had such a hard time believing it. Shock was her constant companion. *He was here one day and gone the next.* Unknown to her, Gustav had appointed a friend of his as guardian of his estate when they had purchased the beer garden, if anything were to happen to him. Born with a keen intelligence and a practical eye for business, Anna snapped out of her grief long enough to realize she was being cheated. How shocked the whole village was when she took this friend to court - and won. But the damage was done, much of the estate was lost overnight, and her darling Alfred had somehow become a man through all of the worry that now sat heavily on his shoulders. So light-hearted when her husband was alive, Alfred's work to keep the business afloat consumed him during economic times that were anything but favorable to the small business owner in Germany. Wars had a way of doing that to most of the economy.

Eric continued talking, perched now on one of the wooden stools that stood near her large rectangular table in the center of the kitchen. *Belgium, Mother, have you ever been there?*

He paused, waiting for her to respond. Wiping her hands along the sides of her striped apron, she looked up with what she hoped was a faint smile.

No, Eric. Always wanted to visit my cousins who live near Antwerp. You'll have to tell me all about it when you return.

She lowered her head to roll out the dough, hoping he didn't hear the slight quiver that had crept into her voice, as if defying her resolve to show nothing of her growing fear. She had tried so hard to keep him safe from the army's reaches.

When he had turned fourteen and high school as a possibility loomed on the horizon, she had inquired about apprenticeships. Working as a chef made good practical sense, given the family's background and businesses. He had always showed an interest in the cooking end of the restaurant while Alfred leaned toward the business end of things. And it had been Eric who spent time with relatives on their farms after his father died, learning how to grow vegetables and raise livestock. Besides that, he idolized his father's brother, his godfather, who was a butcher and often took him for weeks at a time after Gustav died.

Yes, she had thought at the time, *such training could ground him, keep him safe from the army for awhile should war become a way of life here.*

So she had gradually dropped hints about apprenticeships and how good he would be since he loved to cook anyway...

Eric approached her one day as she rolled out her dough in the kitchen.

I really don't want to go to high school, Mother. You know how I love to use my hands and do things for myself. If I were a chef, I could travel and make a decent living and I love to cook! Do you think you could find me an apprenticeship?

And so she did.

He had loved being apprenticed to a chef, she remembered, in an all-girl school at that! He had started out scrubbing pots and pans but soon moved on to preparing vegetables and even slaughtering the animals. What his uncle had taught him in those few years after his father died really helped him, she realized.

Finally she thought he was safe there, until war broke out, and all bets were off. First those finishing high school were recruited, followed by those assigned as apprentices. For many of these youths, as soon as they saw the clean pressed uniforms and witnessed the salute, they would be so anxious to get going ...

Anna looked at her son now as he rambled on about all he had been told at army headquarters. His eyes glistened with the possibilities. How she worried for her youngest! What mother wouldn't? She had followed as best she could what was happening in the world around her. First the news would mention Belgium, then Paris, then what was happening in Poland. Too much! Too much! She thought of her parents and the life they had lived when she was young. She had no memory of the world changing all around her like it seemed to be doing now. Not just for her. But now Eric. He still seemed so young to her with all the enthusiasm he carried for life.

Just let him return home when it's over, just let him return home... Anna prayed along with many a mother in Germany that night as well.

"Auf Wiedersehen, mein lieber sohn, auf wiedersehen."

One day dissolved into the next as weeks passed and these newly inducted troops trudged northwest towards Belgium. Crossing the Rhine was Eric's first encounter with fear. As he watched the part of Germany that meant home to him recede from view, his stomach knotted for the first time. They were moving quickly now. They had been told that they were to sweep through Belgium in order to get to France, encircling Paris.

Sweep? That's what my mother does at the restaurant every day after she's finished preparing the menus and washing the pots and pans. Not this!

This was one of the few times he allowed his thoughts free reign. When on the move like they always were, such a luxury could be the difference between living and dying.

Eric tried to warm himself hunched down by the small fire he and his buddies had finally succeeded in starting. The winds had calmed long enough for the dried grasses to catch and hold. With the constant dampness and frequent movement, it seemed such an extravagance to stay put for one night.

As he thought of his mother, he could see her scuttling from one corner to the next, moving chairs and occasionally bumping into a table, picking up energy as she made her way around the vast open space. Sweeping Belgium was definitely something else entirely! Little by little, he realized as he stayed huddled by the fire, blowing on his finger-tips to get them warm, sarcasm was creeping into the very privacy of his thoughts. Probably born from youth's idealism fast deflating not only for him but so many around him moving now across the fields and towns of Europe, swept up in a military surge like one of those tsunamis that no one can imagine being able to stop. Everything was changing too quickly.

He awoke the next morning to the constant popping of gunfire along with cries of wounded men and fires erupting wherever he looked. As he hurriedly joined others breaking camp, he found himself in a constant state of reaction. To react was to survive.

Keep moving, Eric, keep moving, he kept muttering to himself. And then he saw her. Actually, he heard her crying first. She was bent low in the field they were passing through, trying to shoo away flies from the dead body of her sister. They looked so much alike that they could have been twins, Eric thought to himself. German artillery had felled her by mistake as she was placing potatoes in the basket that now lay next to her. He couldn't take his eyes away; he couldn't move. Life stopped for him then. He stood rooted to the ground that held him upright. Luckily tall grasses kept him hidden. As far as his eyes could see, all was being destroyed - crops, houses, whole villages. At that moment the boy he had been as he left his mother's house vanished, never to return.

As he ran with this surviving child in his arms to a make-shift shelter, he kept thinking:

What is all this for anyway? What had this little girl and her now dead sister done to deserve this? He couldn't make sense out of what anyone was doing. And they just kept marching toward Paris. Something like a prayer formed in his head as he left her with a farmer and hurried to keep up with the others:

If I make it back home, I will start over. Not one day will be wasted. I will never speak of what I've seen here. My life has to mean more than this. That poor little girl is saving me...

Eric did make it back home, but Anna knew immediately it wouldn't be for long. A hardness had settled into his eyes, a resolve. He was changed, changed utterly. So often she would find him just staring into space, yet she couldn't think of anything to say. This remoteness became a part of who he was now. It did seem as if all of Europe was in mourning.

As a soldier, he knew that poison gas and aerial bombing of civilians had been used for the first time in this war. In his mind's eye, he kept seeing a soldier frantically trying to get his gas helmet in place before the yellow air reached his lungs. Fumbling to get it secure, he drowned from the gas, shaking in spasms right before Eric's eyes. It also was the first time that more men died in battle than died from disease. And for what? This was the one question that refused to leave his mind. It was there as soon as he awakened in the morning. It was the last thing he thought about before drifting off to sleep at night.

He tried to put all his energy into helping his mother. He could see her now with new eyes. She seemed so much older to him than when he first left. Germany had gone into serious inflation. The mark was worth next to nothing.

Why it takes a bundle of money just to buy a loaf of bread! Eric muttered to himself as he walked through town. The bushel basket of money he saw in front of the post-master's office was the last straw. *All of this currency and it can buy next to nothing. There's got to be another way...*

When he returned home, Anna prepared for the worst.

I have a job, Mother. A cook on a cruise ship that sails the Atlantic. I need to be aboard in a week's time.

He would take a train north first, buying some necessities when he was closer to the ship.

So don't fuss, heine Mutter, I really can't take anything from here...

Anna knew in her mother's heart that her son was finding his way. What she didn't know then was that he would not be returning to Germany with the ship. When it left from America several weeks into the future, he wouldn't be on board.

What I remember most vividly from that day I walked off the ship was how badly my hands were shaking as I put the last of the dishes away after the evening meal. The ship would set sail during the night. There was a flurry of activity near the kitchen as venders brought the last of the supplies aboard before we would be setting out later in the evening. Now was the time.

I knew it in every fiber of my being. Now - or never. To this day, I honestly don't know if on some unconscious level I had planned it out all along, or whether it happened in one explosive moment of jagged awareness: Now, Eric, NOW!

My mouth was so dry that I had to keep swallowing in order to breathe. I grabbed some boxes and began following some venders who were disembarking. I tried to use their easy chatter floating into the twilight air to soothe my ragged nerves. Talking to myself didn't hurt either. "Stay close enough to look like you're one of them, Eric. Far enough back that you won't be noticed by them. Delicate balance."

Don't race, Eric. Keep your head down. Slowly. Slowly.

As I took that first step onto land, it hit me so forcefully: I was in America. This would be my new home. All things were possible. I stopped myself right there. *Pay attention, Eric. The hardest part is behind you. You made it. Seek cover. Don't let yourself be seen. Survive. Sleep under cover of the night. Tomorrow will be time enough to chart a way forward.*

And with that, army skills came back, helping me navigate my way through New York. I had no trouble finding a job in the Speakeasies on the lower East Side. Living in a cold-water flat didn't bother me at all. I was in America where a willingness to work hard promised a paycheck and a future. Imagine that!

With my first paycheck, I sent word to my mother. How hard this would be for her! Yet I knew that I would be able to send her money now, making life easier, at least in part. In the weeks and months that followed, as luck would have it, my apprenticeship in food training back in Germany really came in handy. How is it possible for that part of my life (which today would be called my teen-age years) seemed so much like a different life-time? I was beginning to see how nothing is ever lost in our lives, that any trade or talent or experience that sets you apart from all the other immigrants arriving daily into New York really counted for something.

My first real break was landing a job as assistant chef on the lower East Side at a place called The Zone Club. My life took on an exciting rhythm in this new country of mine. New friends and I would go to dances on weekends in a place called Astoria in Queens County, beyond the city. Quite a way to travel, my friends told me, but a little taste of home, if only for a few hours a week. From what I was beginning to see, here in America, too, Germans stayed with Germans, Irish with Irish, Italians with Italians. To hear accordion sounds with old German dance tunes meant my feet wouldn't leave the dance floor for those hours that flew by like minutes.

On one of those weekends, I was introduced to Paula Groenekamp who came from Bremerhaven, Germany. What a small world even America was proving itself to be! Eventually we married and every couple of years I moved to other food establishments until I managed to secure an executive chef position at a large business in Brooklyn. I was not afraid to take risks, to cook for larger and larger numbers of people, maxing out at 1000 meals for a lunch-time crowd. Whatever I was asked to take on, I did ; whether I had the experience or not. I wasn't afraid to ask for help from other immigrants who came before me ; after all, every one of us was just trying to find our way forward in this new land where every day it seemed we were introduced to something different from what we had experienced growing up in Germany or elsewhere. I uncovered skills I didn't even know I possessed, handling other workers as well as purchasing foods in vast quantities. I surprised myself by being a good judge of character as well. I knew what to look for in hiring new employees. If they weren't ready to do all that I had done ... no job!

Paula and I were a good team. I loved to tease her over the years:

You only married me because I had my own vacuum cleaner! We agreed on the big things. We didn't allow German to be spoken in our home. We felt everyone in America should speak the same language. Sometimes we forgot that when we were fighting and choice German vocabulary would bounce off one wall right into another!

Becoming what was called at that time "naturalized" citizens was important to both of us. We had both filed first papers which simply stated our intent to become citizens here. Important steps had to be followed before receiving final papers, which would grant citizenship. These involved mastering enough of the language that we could survive here - whether reading signs on buses or in supermarkets telling us what was on sale, or being able to count money correctly when receiving change from purchases. How carefully I practiced reading the Pledge of Allegiance before going down to City Hall for my tests. I can still remember how proud I felt when I was "sworn in" as a citizen and handed my official papers. I had taken such care to follow all the steps leading from filing first papers until now, including the residency requirement at that time. After all, I did get off to a shaky start!

Once Paula and I bought our own home, I worked seven days a week for many years. I was so proud of our family, of what the two of us had accomplished here. Paula loved being a homemaker in this country. She took such pride in tending her gardens, spending hours on her knees in the yard digging, planting, weeding. I can still hear her sobs the morning she came running to me:

Eric, look what someone did. How could they? How could they?

Under cover of night, someone had painted our white picket fence with black swastikas. I had surprised her on her birthday with this extravagant addition for her prized gardens. She was inconsolable until I convinced her that here in America the two of us could paint it back to life again. And we did. Being German in America during the years of World War II and immediately following wasn't always easy, don't get me wrong. But just like painting that fence together, we always worked hard, knowing that in time all else would follow. It was my dear mother, Anna, who taught me that so many years ago back in Germany when my father died. Life wasn't meant to be easy. We would make it here. Look how far we had come. After all, this was America!

⚜ ⚜ ⊰●⊱ ⚜ ⚜

Years later, Peter Fuhrmann, Eric's son, had this to say about his father's decision to leave ship and enter the country the way he did, when he did:

He made that decision based on the circumstances shaping his life at the time. Who could possibly fault him for it? Least of all, his family...

Family/Historical Facts

- Eric's childhood, apprenticeship

- Induction into Army ; March through Belgium

- photograph of Kazimiera Mika mourning the body of her sister*

- illegal entry into country from ship ; employment history

- marriage to Paula Groenekamp

- naturalization papers - 1944

- what happened to the white picket fence

*Author's note:

According to family, there was a marked change in Eric upon returning home from the war. When coming across this picture while researching through pictorial archives for WW1 in Belgium, I allowed this to provide a fictional circumstance that could so influence this young soldier that he would never speak of what he had seen.

For many returning from war, now as well as then, what they have witnessed while being in such an environment influences their actions from that time on.

Genia Ingber
age 21
1939
Poland

I met Genia's daughter, Ida Rabinowitz, over
40 years ago in a high school lunchroom
where we both taught. Over the course of
a lunch period, she told me her mother's
story. "Oh, Ida, this story must be told!" So,
with Ida's help and permission, here it is!

Last Stop: Kostanay

Twenty-one year old Genia Ingber and her family lived in the town of Tomaszow-Lubelski in the Lublin province of eastern Poland. A tiny jewel of a town sedately rooted in a fertile valley equidistant from verdant forests to the east and a series of lakes both large and small encircling its remaining borders like glittering stones in a tiara. Her brothers, mother, and father along with herself worked as laborers in the different trades for which the town was known: tailoring, inn-keeping, weaving, and the many mills dotting the hillsides where grains from outlying farms were brought to be milled and shipped all over Europe. It was, known at this time, 1939, as Europe's breadbasket.

Their house was of modest size, similar to the other houses on the outskirts of town; but with someone always leaving for work when someone else was arriving home from a shift, it never seemed cramped. Genia loved the way the flowers of late summer framed the entrance along with the low-lying green bushes situated on either side of the walk.

But today was different. Pre-occupied with her own dark thoughts, she didn't look up as she swung open the gate, letting the latch fend for itself behind her.

Somehow I've got to make Papa see that we must leave, all of us, right away. Not next week, not after we sell all our belongings, but tonight, as soon as we have the cover of dark. He must listen to me!

She had always been her father's favorite, she knew. With her dark wavy hair and dark eyes, there could be no doubt as to whose daughter she was. Similarities ended there, however. Taciturn by nature and slow to arrive at decisions that affected the family (so much to consider), the elder Ingber often found himself at odds with this daughter whose disposition was entirely opposite from his own.

I must stay calm and reasonable, I must. Our future rides on this, I just know it, Genia thought to herself as she absently went about the kitchen setting the table for an early dinner. As destiny would have it, this was the one day of the week that if they moved dinner up an hour all members of the family could sit down together for a meal.

If I can convince Abraham, he'll help bring Papa around, I know it.

He was the brother closest in age to Genia, looking enough like her to be a twin. Two peas in the same pod were the words often jokingly used by villagers when seeing them together. Similar temperaments, too; but because he was older, and male, his explosions were more tolerated than hers.

Everything hinges on my being able to win Abraham over. The rest will follow if he and Papa agree to what I've learned. I must be sure-footed about this. I must...

⊷ ⊶⟨⊙⟩⊶ ⊷

Genia had a right to be so concerned. Earlier in the day while at work at the inn located in the heart of town, two well-dressed businessmen came in, looking for lodging for the next two days. She had been working unobtrusively at the sewing machine in the far corner of the inn's large foyer. On most days she loved working here repairing linens, tucked away as it were from demanding patrons. Something about their manner, however, a nervous energy of sorts evidenced by one drumming his fingers absent-mindedly on the top of the counter while the other kept looking out the window facing the main street as if he would eventually behold the nightmare he was desperately seeking to avoid. But it was snatches of their conversation that almost instantly riveted her attention.

Are you absolutely sure of your brother's message? the shorter of the two inquired of his companion. *Deserting the bank with no advance notice, we can kiss our positions good-bye, you know...*

But at least we'll be alive! the other retorted with a voice rising in tone, as his companion grabbed hold of his arm.

Keep your voice down, you idiot. We don't want to draw attention. We can catch our breath here until we figure out our next move. Tell me again - slowly- exactly what your brother said.

That the Germans were steadily moving east, crossing into Poland yesterday. Many are being killed... are being confiscated for the army. He wasn't certain if this was befalling everyone or just the Jews, but chaos seems to be following them. He almost screamed over the line Get out Josef while you can, run! Then the line went dead.

Genia sat paralyzed, trying to take in what she had just heard. Granted they lived in eastern Poland, but really how much difference was that going to make in the long run? She decided against questioning the men. Rumors had been running rampant for the past month anyway about what was happening with the growing army in Germany. Right down to her toes, she felt that the words she heard had been true. Searingly raw, but true. What's more, she knew she was meant to hear them.

Grandmother always told me to trust that inner voice. "Genia," she'd say, "That's all we've got in this life, but it's enough..."

With that, Genia found the manager in charge, made her case for being ill, and hurriedly left for the remainder of the day. As she turned the corner, she couldn't resist turning around for one last glimpse of the quaint lattice-trimmed inn she had grown to love.

if things turn out tonight as they must, I might never see you again...

And with that, she hurriedly half-ran the rest of the way home.

Luckily for them, only a thin sliver of moon was visible above the mountains that night. They left with only the clothes on their backs, one suitcase they would take turns carrying, the few "groshen" they kept in a crock behind the stove pipe in the kitchen for emergencies, and any coins or bills that might have been in anyone's pockets.

Better to be safe and alive, Genia heard her father half-mutter under his breath as he left, locking the door behind him.

He suddenly looks so old, Genia thought as she waited for him to come down the path. His shoulders looked stooped; he appeared to be almost shuffling along the walkway.

Will he even be able to walk through these forests into Russia? What will we do if he can't walk anymore? Slow down, Genia, she tried to assure herself. *One step at a time, girl. We've passed the first hurdle. We're on our way.*

Unknown to them at the time, the vast majority of Polish Jews who survived the Holocaust owe their survival to their flight to the Soviet Union. That didn't mean that all was well when they eventually arrived there. They found work in the fields where they met up with others who, like them, had fled and now were desperate for work of any kind. Resentment could be seen in the faces of the Russian peasants who like them worked so hard for so little. Arriving in such numbers, they were even being called "class aliens."

They're not very friendly, are they? Genia remarked one day to her mother while working side by side gathering a late harvest.

Careful, Genia, keep your remarks to yourself. You never know who could be listening or why.

It wasn't long after that Genia regretted not taking her mother's admonition to heart. She had been sent to work alongside a girl about her own age. In an attempt to start up a conversation, Genia remarked,

At least in Germany at the end of a week we'd have a few groshen left over to buy some sugar or butter. Here there isn't any to buy even if you did have the extra coins.

It was the next day that she was summoned to the manager's trailer.

It has come to our attention that you are a spy for the Germans, and a confession was placed in front of her to sign.

What are you talking about? My family and I fled from the Germans! Genia screamed back at this face sitting in front of her.

You were overheard in the fields yesterday complaining about your life here. You must have been sent.

I'm not signing anything. I'm no spy...

It doesn't matter if you sign or not! he retorted. *You are being sentenced to three years in Siberia either way.*

Too much too soon. As the train chugged through the mountains, Genia collapsed into a corner. She couldn't stop sobbing. How could this be happening? The train was filled with others going to prison as well who laughed at her, calling her a baby.

Three years? Why that's nothing. Most of us are sentenced to hard labor for 15 years. A few get the prize for 20! The others laughed at the attempt to get her to lighten up. Seriously, little sister, start now learning to save your strength...

When she stepped off the train in Siberia, she couldn't believe what she was seeing. Desolation. Gone were the vibrant forests. No green anywhere. For as far as the eye could see, no vegetation. The entrance ways to the coal mines were the bleakest of all - gaping holes in the crust of the earth. Once inside, no sunlight for 8-10 hours at a clip. The camps where the workers lived, no better. No warm clothing was issued, no shoes, only rags to wrap around the soles of their feet. As for food, Genia decided early on to trade away her one bowl of soup a day for an additional piece of bread. It kept her stomach quiet longer and that seemed to help.

In many lives, at one time or another, Destiny quietly enters and holds out a gentle hand. And that's what happened to Genia on a day that looked as bleak as any other.

Just as she was stepping into the car that would bring her deep into the mine, she collapsed. When she regained consciousness, she found out that she had been operated on for a bleeding ulcer. Unlike at the mines or the prison camp, the people here were friendly, especially the doctor and nurses.

So tell us, Genia, what's happening out there? We get no news here at all.

Genia began laughing. *Now where should I begin?*

In no time at all, this curly haired, dark eyed beauty became everyone's favorite. She had such a capacity to adapt to her surroundings and more importantly, make herself indispensable to those who worked here. Remember, she could sew. The doctor remarked one day how much his back was bothered by the cold. Genia gathered some pelts from the storage rooms and painstakingly sewed a coat by hand for him. He was so appreciative that he kept renewing the form for additional healing time for her when officials inquired from the prison camp.

Being kept out of the mines for the rest of her sentence probably saved her life. When her sentence was up, she was still at the hospital. One day an officer in a green uniform arrived to issue her dismissal papers.

To what city in Russia do you wish to be sent? The officer stopped writing for the moment and looked up at her.

Genia thought quickly. She only knew of two big cities.

Moscow. She tried to sound sure of herself, in charge of her life from here on out.

Nyet. He barked back at her with a brutal finality.

Without missing a beat, Genia matched his tone with *Leningrad,* the only other city in Russia she had heard of.

Nyet was out of his mouth before her last syllable had been uttered.

With a clear insight borne of a panic that surely she would be left behind at the prison, Genia knew she had to pick Siberia.

She remembered hearing hospital staff joking about what other way would Russia be able to populate such a barren region if not for the people whose sentences were up? No one in their right mind would choose to live where nothing seemed destined to grow. Just months before, a journalist from the camp had been admitted to the hospital for appendicitis. In one of their talks, she had mentioned to Genia that her release was imminent and she was going to Kostanay in Siberia.

Kostanay! Genia shouted to the officer whose face registered such surprise that someone would volunteer to go to such a place that Genia almost laughed. With a final stamp to her papers, Genia was free to be on the next train out the following morning at 9:45 a.m.

She could hardly contain her excitement when she boarded the train and saw so many people filling the seats. All different ages and sizes, talking and laughing. For one fleeting instant, she thought she spotted her mother ahead of her already seated until the woman turned to the man next to her and her face became more clearly visible.

Oh Mama, will I ever see you again? she allowed herself the luxury of holding this thought for the length of time it took her to pass by the woman in the aisle.

Enough, Genia. That is enough. If it's meant to be, it will be.

She thought of her no more. Genia had hardened over these three years. On some level she knew her survival depended on keeping familial emotion way down deep for safe-keeping. Someday she would think of them again, but not today.

Once seated, she willed herself to take in the changing landscape. At each stop, people exited. At first busy little towns and then long stretches of open spaces, few buildings, fewer trees. When the last two people exited the train, the conductor called out, *Last stop, Kostanay,* and she steeled herself once again for what was about to meet her.

As soon as the train braked for this last stop, the doors automatically opened and cold winds wrapped themselves around Genia's bare legs. As she descended the steel stairs, the brutal cold seared into the soles of her feet through the makeshift rag coverings taking the place of shoes. She could hardly bear taking that last step from train to hard-packed snow. With only a short-sleeved dress on and no employment document that would allow her to go into any commercial establishment either to eat or find lodging, she hobbled into a phone booth near-by.

Curled up on the floor of this cramped space, she folded her head into her arms, resting both along the tiny seat. *Oh, dear God, what am I going to do?* Only now, hidden from view, did Genia allow herself to indulge in tears.

Suddenly the door behind her started to move, as if someone was trying to enter.

One minute, I'll be right out, she called without turning around. She quickly wiped her face with the back of her hands and attempted to get herself up from the floor. For one quick second, Genia thought she might burst into laughter. Facing her as she exited the booth was a slightly rotund man with a grin extending from one rather large ear to the other. One hand had hastily removed a cap, revealing a slightly balding head. As her eyes met his, he bowed slightly as if she might be visiting royalty.

Welcome to Kostanay. My name is Jonas Fisch. I work in the gas station across from where the train stops and I saw you arrive. You must be cold.

And with that, he took off his jacket and wrapped it around her shoulders. She had all she could do not to burst into sobs that she knew she would never be able to stop. Such a simple gesture, such an overt act of kindness now held the power to totally undo her. He brought her over to the gas station where she could sit before a small fire inside. He offered her his seat, a small, three-legged stool, while he poured her a cup of hot tea.

You come from the prison camp, don't you, he uttered with the tone of one who knows truth when he runs into it. *I, too, was sent here. I'm Jewish and I'm Polish and I had been heard saying that Russian tools were primitive, and they didn't like being insulted, I guess. So after a three year stint in the mines, I was allowed to resettle here.*

By now he had returned to stand near her and the fire. *I was lucky enough to find work here and I rent a room from a family just down the street.* With that, he gestured toward a small house barely visible from the small cracked window to the right of the door.

Perhaps it was love at first sight.

Perhaps it was a trust in the goodness of another borne after years of knowing none.

Perhaps it was the ability to still listen to that inner voice that her grandmother told her always to rely on, now telling her *survive, Genia, survive.*

Or, like so many decisions that lay claim to our lives, a combination of some or all of the above.

So when Jonas, in the course of that long conversation told her about his sister in America and told her that one day he would take her there if she would marry him, her heart never missed a beat.

Yes, Jonas, I will marry you...

Genia's daughter Ida speaks:

I was born in 1944 while my parents were still in Kostany. They worked as a team: my mother managed to barter sugar for goods ; and my father, for extra money, the kerosene he was able to get from the place where he worked. This is how they survived until they saved enough to get back to Poland. Russia repatriated all Polish citizens in 1945. My mother was reunited with one of her brothers and my grandmother when they returned to Poland. My father's family (nine siblings) had been killed by the Nazi's. Only his sister in America survived.

As for my mother's large family? One brother served in the Russian army, moving to Australia after the war. Another brother stayed in Poland until much later, then America in 1972. Her mother and brother who had stayed in Poland emigrated to Israel in 1952, when anti-Semitism showed itself once again, so they left Poland. What happened to her family is a perfect example of what the history books have called the Polish - Jewish Diaspora. America - Australia - Israel - scattered like seeds in the wind all over the globe. One family who once lived under the same roof, ate the same meals, laughed, talked, argued even - who, through no fault of their own, became displaced from the town they had called home. They were Polish and Jewish, and Poland had become a pawn in World War II.

We came to America in 1948, sponsored by his sister, which meant that someone promised the government that there was a place for them to live and a job for them to go to when they arrived. That was the definition for legal immigration at that time.

My father kept his promise to that young girl he met that day so long ago when her world seemed so hopeless. Their story is sad, that is true ; but they survived and that is such a good thing! Here I am now, telling you this amazing story of survival from a time when millions of others just like them weren't as lucky. It has been estimated that 20% of the Polish population - 3 million Jews - were killed during World War II.

The older I get, I stand in awe of that young girl who, getting off a train in Kostany, Siberia, found within her the strength to risk her future by placing her life in the hands of a stranger, who then brought the three of us to America - just like he said he would.

Family/Historical Facts

- Polish history of the period

- the flight of Genia and her family in 1939

- use of term class aliens

- circumstances surrounding coal mining, hospital stay, charges brought against her, prison sentence

- train ride to Kostany

- Genia's meeting with Jonas; his proposal

- members of family- aftermath

Author's note:

I took the liberty of providing a possible scenario that fit the only fact available to me -

"they fled.". It is amazing to me how human lives, if motivated strongly enough, have the power to just walk (or run) away with nothing but the clothes on their backs and each other. Fear, to me, is one of the most powerful motivators of all. Hence, the fictional account of the two young men...

It is generally believed that 350,000 - 400,000 citizens fled eastward ahead of the German invasion. The majority of the Polish-Jewish remnant survived only because they did so.

Afterword

Now you've met them: John, Eric, Sadie, and Genia - all young with their lives stretching ahead of them, all with close family ties, even though their countries of origin were different. Four among thousands who were faced with unalterable choices. Being who they were, they opted for America, and never looked back.

While writing their stories, I found myself drawn to the plight of their parents: Michael (John's father), Anna (Eric's mother), and dear Benjamin (Sadie's father) specifically. In the days of these events, both parents and children knew they would most probably never see each other again. How bad do situations have to be in order for a parent to make such a decision - or give their approval, at the very least?

According to the Pew Research Center, in the year 2015, 17,500 unaccompanied minors from Honduras were apprehended at our border, to give just one example. Can you imagine how desperate parents must be to send children on without them to another country?

War, like a vast contagion, covers many lands in our world today - the Middle East, Africa, Central and South America. Homes, schools, neighborhoods - all destroyed. As of this writing, vast numbers of refugees are roaming to and through Europe from points further east and south, looking for a place to live without war. Here in America, they continue to be found near our borders. It stands to reason that not all who want to enter America can do so. Articles are being written and politicians are running for office on platforms addressing the complex issue of immigration, both legal and illegal.

Another vast contagion is fear. With each terrorist attack, no matter where in the western world it occurs, mounting fear of whoever is different from us - whether in nationality or religion or even in the clothes they wear - seems to grow in exponential proportions. New conditions to be met for entry into America are currently being introduced into an already complex system called the Vetting Process. This process can take up to two years to complete, making America's one of the most thorough in the world. How careful we are trying to be while remaining true to the ideals that laid the foundation for this grand experiment of "We the People..." begun in 1776, supported with the rule of law - our Constitution, in 1789, and re-iterated so eloquently by Abraham Lincoln after the Civil War almost tore it apart in 1865.

But for those who eventually come to America like the four young people you've read about? Remember they, too, came with stories that called forth steady courage to make choices that must have been heart-wrenching. They, along with all of us, will be part of shaping what America will look like and be like in this century, much in the same way that John and Eric and Sadie and Genia and millions of others like them shaped 20th century America with its values, cultures, customs, problems, and the solutions for many of those problems.

A young poet named Emma Lazarus who lived in New York City at the beginning of the twentieth century spent much of her time helping the refugees who were pouring into the country. She was inspired to give words to Lady Liberty's silent presence greeting all who entered into the harbor. She called her the Mother of Exiles in a poem entitled "The New Colossus" which contained the following words:

> *"Give me your tired, your poor*
> *your huddled masses yearning to breathe free*
> *the wretched refuse of your teeming shore.*
> *Send these, the homeless, tempest-tossed to me*
> *I lift my lamp beside the golden door."*

And in giving her a voice, she reminded America of its unique identity. One cannot see that statue even now, almost a century later, without hearing at the same time those words inscribed on its base as a mandate to all of us.

Didn't Senator Edward Kennedy, in a speech given at the Democratic National Convention in 2008, bring our attention back to that same mandate?

> *"The work goes on,*
> *the hope still lives...*
> *and the dream shall never die."*

We, and the America we are continually becoming, simply need to carry on...

Historical Background

Brownstone, David. *Island of Hope, Island of Tears.* New York: Fall River Press, 1979.

Ferguson, Niall. *The Pity of War - Explaining WWI.* New York: Basic Books, 1999.

Follett, Ken. *The Fall of the Giants* (first of Century Trilogy) New York: Penguin Group, 2010. *The Winter of Our World* (second of Century Trilogy), 2012.

Kelly, Joanna. *Hooligan's Alley.* IN: I Universe, 2013.

Kelly, Mary Pat. *Galway Bay.* New York: Grand Central Publishing, 2009. *Of Irish Blood.* Forge/ Macmillan, 2015.

Marriot, Sir J.A.R. *A History of Europe 1815 - 1939.* New York: Barnes & Noble, Inc., 1963.

Weinzierl, Erika. *The Jewish Middle Class in Vienna Late 19th and Early 20th Century*, working paper,01 - 1, October, 2003.

Made in the USA
Middletown, DE
30 July 2020